Y0-DKN-934

The Immigrant's House

Also by Rob Smith:

Poetry:
Mzungu, Hello: a Poetic Journal (color chapbook)
256 Zones of Gray

Novels:
Children of Light
McGowan's Call
McGowan's Retreat
McGowan's Return
Night Voices (now included as Book I in *Keelhouse*)
Shrader Marks: Keelhouse

Literary criticism and commentary:
Cultural Perspectives on the Bible: A Beginner's Guide
Hogwarts, Narnia, and Middle Earth: Places Upon a Time

Tween's literature:
The Spell of Twelve

The Immigrant's House

Rob Smith

Drinian Press/
Huron, Ohio

The Immigrant's House
Smith, Robert Bruce

Copyright © 2012 by Robert Bruce Smith. All rights reserved. Except for use in a review, no part of this book may be reproduced or utilized in any form or by any means electronic or mechanical without permission of the author.

Photos: Rob Smith,
Cover: marabou stork at Nakuru, Kenya

Drinian Press LLC
PO Box 63
Huron, Ohio 44839

Online at www.DrinianPress.com.

Acknowledgements:
"I spit in the river like a boy" received the 2006 Robert Frost Poetry Award and was published online by the Frost Foundation of Lawrence, MA.

Poems in the section "256 Zones of Gray" are taken largely from a volume by the same name, published by Bird Dog Publishing, Huron, Ohio and used by permission of the author and copyright holder. ©2008 Robert Bruce Smith

Library of Congress Control Number: 2012941722

ISBN-10: 0-9833069-4-X
ISBN-13: 978-0-9833069-4-8

Printed in the United States of America

Contents

The Immigrant's House

Kenya: *Mzungu, hello*

256 Zones of Gray

"Earth"

The Immigrant's House

They confessed that they were strangers and foreigners on this earth, and by so doing, they made it clear that they were looking for a country, a homeland.

Hebrews 11:13, 14

There was a time when
German was spoken
in my house,
but not by anyone I know.
They spoke in these rooms before new drywall
wore pictures of lighthouses
and boats mooring in protected waters.

At night, when darkness
takes away the colored walls,
I listen for the words of
sermons practiced
for a pulpit down the street.
Spoken to a people who remembered
the cholera, the burning,
and newspapers in English
telling of twelve dead:
    two strangers
        six Germans,
and four others with names printed below.

This house was their home,
as they set out each morning,
navigating streets with Noah Webster's tongue
weighed down by heavy consonants.
On Sunday, they *sprecht Deutsch*
to a God who understood human hearts.
The language of that devotion
is gone from this town,
though the immigrant fear remains.
I hear its echoes at night alone
in the questions that stand stronger than answers,
Was ist dein einiger trost in leben und in sterben?[*]
What is your only trust in life and in death?

---

[*] The first question of the Heidelberg Catechism

Two Poets

I met a friend
at breakfast.
The server poured
coffee, then
asked six times if
the food was okay.
Coffee is warmed
again
and I will have
caffeine shakes
before our time is up.

We pull words
between us,
borrowed words,
words older than
ourselves and
into which
we pour our
life's meaning.

I can't imagine
a time
when the saying
would be over,
no longer staking
pilfered words
to new meaning
between bites
of scrambled eggs
and the smell
of coffee.

"Is everything okay here?"
That's seven.
We will leave
an extra couple bucks.

Breakfast tips don't pay
the rent on our booth
or her house,
but neither do
the words
that become
the poet's life.

The Boxer

Still walks with swagger
of swinging arms
bowed out
by invisible
biceps
lifting them from
his ribcage.

He is the
fighter
he always was,
or thought he
was,
and the waitress
smiled politely.
He knew
she wanted
the tough guy
hidden
beneath droopy
eyelids
and receding hair.

"The pretty ones go for the thugs,"
he puffs
and his voice
gets louder.
Then she's gone.

The cantaloupes are ripe now
having taken the
early downpours
and wrapped brown husks
over
sweet fruit.
I brought one home
and it sat in a
brown bag until
the smell warmed
the kitchen.
A single slice
released golden seeds
in a free falling
clump.

It spooned like pudding.
And from the empty
rind, I drank
the last
drops of the spring rain.

Sister

When mother went away
to care for the baby,
sister took charge.
It was the way it had to be
with little brothers, and
mother being so soon
gone.
Father was busy
working numbers,
but seeing only dead ends.
Strong children rise
to needs unspoken knowing
that at the center of a house is a place
to run when dreams
turn dark,
or teacher says "Everyone, remember
to take your pictures home,
the ones you made for your mothers."
Such a simple thing,
but she went away to care for the baby never seen,
and school art was loaded into a dresser drawer
till sister would bring out her
drawings to lay
side by side
in a children's gallery
seen by no adult eyes.
It was the best she could arrange.
It was the way it had to be
with mother so far away.

Cormorants

Blue sky over blue-green water
and a Crayola-yellow sun. My teacher,
with brown crayon and practiced flick,
set a checkmark against a cloud
and called it a bird.

It was!

And with speed of flight, I took the wax stick
and released a flock to fill the sky
with little vees
flying home,
or away,
or out of the two dimensions of my page.

In physics, my professor drew a bird,
but called it vector.
Magnitude and direction
becoming velocity
pointing to the edge of the graph paper.

Why?

To escape? To fly? To become a bird?

And in the world of up and down and away,
a vector passes overhead until it becomes
checkmarks,
a vee of vees,
cormorants flying silently,
not like the cranky geese.
These fly with unsounded purpose,
magnitude and direction becoming
velocity running off the page
of the world.

Tangerines, easy to peel,
yielding
to little fingers
as if the pungent rind could not bear
the soft touch of the fruit.
Always leaping free
at first puncture of
dimpled end.
It was orange, but not orange,
with sections that fooled only
eye, not mouth.
Dry and sweet without the tartness that quenches,
not orange.

Oranges would not surrender so easily.
I watched my father to see it done.
He would bite the bitter end,
or force back an opening with the side of a spoon.
Once cracked,
fingers pried
burrowing and pulling,
fighting grip of juicy pulp.
In the end,
the pieces of the shell
were big and few
and the fruit worth the price of any sting of small cuts.

Last night,
at the end of my fingers,
I saw my father's hands
open an orange.
Still a perfect gift.

Mornings
we'd sweep the ash
off the back stoop
and see yellow haze
over the Ohio
pressing down around
Brown's Island.

Walking Third Street to coffee,
the valley smell took me
again to high school—
the day senior boys
burned sulfur near the science room,
and then to
summer's first cold gulp
of rotten-egg water spouting
from a galvanized pipe
at church camp.

"That's the smell of money,"
the old locals would say between sips
from stained Shenango Pottery cups
drawn up from brown rings
on square white paper napkins.

For them, good times
never
meant blue skies—
And at night
the really dirty coal
burned darkly over the
power plant and football field.

Seemed a fair trade—
lung tissue for groceries.

Hard to measure the
loss of sky
when there's a taste of money
in the mouth.

November

In November,
the seagulls come
flowing with
wind over the water
from Canada
to the corn fields,
foraging among the stubble
of freshly cut stalks.
The crows,
having taken flight,
give over this broader shoreline
for the fish-fed cousins
who nibble and squawk
until Odysseus returns
carrying an oar
to complete his repentance
and send them home
to the sea.

Thanksgiving Parade

My ears
were not ready when
the marching band
hit a blaring
downbeat.
The tune was
"Simple Gifts," now
tempoed for a
march
as if
an army of pacifists
had taken
a sudden
militant turn.
Such a plain tune
fully ornamented
rising above
all heads
and still upward,
up to where
Garfield and Snoopy
romped
to break free
from the puny
humans straining
on string leashes.
At the sound,
dead Shakers
turned.

Bird Watching

If we put out fish sticks,
would the seagulls
come to the birdfeeder?
Thistles bring finches,
sunflowers, the cardinals
peanuts,
jays and squirrels,
but would a
carp
tempt the gulls
off the lake, or
a shiner
a great blue?

From the back porch
we hear the
waves at night
and live at the junction of two worlds.
It's the swallows,
diving for dragonflies and midges
over wave and lawn
that become the
conjunction
joining each to
the other.

Angles, straight lines
and an image following
on black marble
jump
through glass onto the
disapproving face of a mannequin,
bikinied and pointing to
a poster-beach in Cancun.
Pigeon droppings on concrete meet
hot asphalt at the curb,
and a yellow stripe tells me not
to cross. It's not my place.
Still, the city poets mock a world
of curving lines and bending
horizons with churning whitecaps
or jagged teeth.
My world is as asymmetrical
as my ears
and the honey locust on the corner
twists in the wind.
"Oaks and maples are the same,"
they tell me,
"a tree is a tree is a tree."
In the city I forget
myself
and could believe the mannequin
face
and become a ghost under glass
in this hard place,
but my legs ache to run
to take rest under a maple,
not an oak,
away from
straight lines
that are not human.

Cell Phone

Who do they talk to,
these living-dead with vacant expressions
and animated voices?
Is it someone a block away
also trapped by an electronic ear muff,
speaking with equal urgency,
each living in dread of the empty silence
of thought?
I should not judge so harshly.
Perhaps they are guiding a pilotless plane
to a life-saving landing,
or transferring countless sums of money
for humanitarian aid.
What is wrong with me
that I have no one to tell
that I am going to the bathroom now?

Muffleheads

Around here,
we call them "muffleheads;"
outsiders say "midges."
Everyone swings and flails
passing through the hoards,
cursing their springtime onslaught.
But, they do not bite or sting!
They look only for sex,
a high calling for such little bugs
whose younger siblings
fed the fish that
fed the humans
who now swear
and swat them aside.

Booted and shoveled,
I set out to plant a tree,
but the first overturned sod
stopped me.
With blade aimed
to break the clump,
a single stone
turned my resolve.

Touched before,
this triangle flaked
to razor edge
set my hand trembling
as I reached out.

Handed across time
with the sound of bowstring
over hundreds of years,
    to me,
        in this place.

I wonder who shaped it
and for what purpose
deer or rabbit,
    dinner or defense.
All I know is the feel of the flint
and the strength of the earth
    that held it.

The one who loosed the dart
stood here,
    or nearby.
Though sharing no time,
we stand in this place
together.

Today we bury
tokens,
setting time and place
for future hands
to open and touch.

What will they think?

Will we be
quaint,
     familiar,
          or odd?

Will their hands quiver
to touch the things
we touched,
to know we were here,
and share,
over time,
a place we love. *

---

* Composed for the dedication of a *Bicentennial Time Capsule* during the poet's
tenure as the city's poet laureate

Huron Before

Before the train
whistled the town awake,
before the church bells rang
or news was spoken at the donut shop,
before sailors and fishermen,
before ore boats and railroad spurs,
before the shipbuilders,
the Wyandot,
Iroquois, and
Huron,
before human eye or ear,
this Cat pawed at the shores.
"Our shores,"
we've claimed them.
But after our eyes and ears
grow dim and
our words and clatter
have ended,
it will still leave tracks
on the sands of Lakefront and
along the Nickel Plate,
as it pulls water down the river
thirsting to
remember a territory
older than time.[*]

---

[*] "Erie" is the shortened form of the Native American word "Erielhonan" meaning "long tail". It is used in reference to wild cats and the people the early French explorers called *Nation Du Chat*. Those who live near the lake know that it still lives up to its wildcat reputation. Written for the City of Huron in its bicentennial year during the poet's tenure as the city's poet laureate

Past the light,
along the breakwall
where Great Blues
pose in stillness,
gulls mount
white limestone hills,
and cormorants
stretch wet wings
to the warm sun.
The river welcomes,
and though it winds back
into the country,
        to farmlands
                and fields,
here it kisses the lake,
and Huron meets Erie.
Today the Cat purrs in
the sunshine of home,
Red Right Returning.
Returning home. *

---

* *Red Right Returning* is an essential rule of navigation. Boats returning from a larger body of water keep the red markers on their right to stay in the safe channel. The Huron Light is a red beacon. Written for the City of Huron in its bicentennial year during the poet's tenure as the city's poet laureate.

cold wind shakes branches,
bright colors rustle the day
as a season breaks.

wind shaking
colors the day,
a season breaks

color
breaks
time

full moon by daylight
shimmers against deep blue,
lace upon sky

daylight moon
sky shimmering
lace

moon
sky
lace

Kenya: *Mzungu, hello*

The earth is one.
This place so far from home,
home.

This section comes from a poetic journal written in western Kenya in January of 2012. During that time, I saw two Africas, the one of the safari tourists, and the one of the people of the Eldoret region. The two are distinctly different, intersecting in a land of immense beauty and populated by a resourceful and resilient people.

RBS

Mzungu

I dress like the locals
but can't get the
skin right,
so they call me
mzungu and stare. [*]

---

[*] *Mzungu* is Kiswahili for *foreigner*, but is now often used to mean "white person". In Eldoret in western Kenya, *wazungu* (pl.) are both a rarity and an alien presence.

We killed our Christmas poinsettia.
It was a gift from a friend, but
the cat started
nibbling,
and it went,
one sunny day,
to the back porch,
but I forgot, and the cold night
took it.

The one here
in the yard
by the basketball hoop
seems a tree
mocking my forgetfulness
as it towers
over me.
Its twenty blooms,
in unison,
ask after their
cousin in Ohio.

Crows

Their voices sound
the same, but
these Kenyan cousins
wear white
vests
squabbling
over seed pods
on top of
a neighbor's tree.

At home
cawing announces
spring,
but here,
in African summer,
spring seems
a long way
away.

Before Sunrise

Lines of running shapes
move along
well-footed ruts
framing the
road like
shadows
of a dim dawn
streaming into
towns inhaling
their first breath
of day.

The best stores
are tucked
off the street
and burst
with handcrafted
treasures of
wood, soapstone, and weaving.
The prices are
modest to my eyes,
but I do not count shillings
as a local
and walk the two blocks
from the ATM at Barclays
to the arcade
safely under
watch of the
blue uniforms
cradling
AK47s.

Eldoret Night

At night they close the
black grillwork over the
front door. It clangs shut
ending with a solemn
click.
Only the first night alarming, soon
becoming the ritual sound of darkness
signaling sleep soon to come
to a house
gated in a cluster of gated houses
sealed round by cinderblock walls
topped with electrified barbed wire,
surrounded again with
another gated perimeter–
and making my bed the inner doll
of a *Matryoshka*,
where I sleep
free in Africa
with three iron gates
and three block walls
between me and the street
where tomorrow bundles
of old clothes and shoes
will be spilled out
on the dirt pathway for sale,
and I will walk past without need,
trying not to see,
never tempted to buy.

But tonight, the dogs
inside the compound walls
bark me awake.
Are they just talking to the guards,
practicing,
or do they see desperate
shadows on the wall?
I wonder as I sleep
free in Africa.

People were butchered
in Burnt Forest after the last
election with
houses and schools
and lives
brought to dust.
Now new roofs of
corrugated steel
mark the places of
fire and machete,
shining like tombstones
under a Kenyan sun.
Still the politicians
who stole the ballots
and stoked the
flames of death
stand again for election
even as their crimes
are enumerated at
The Hague.
This is the day,
the court announces.
The army is on the streets
of Burnt Forest.
Wazungu are on lockdown;
the country holds its breath.

Twiga

What is so odd
that you look
at us
over the
acacia
where you lick
green leaves
off thorny branches?
Do you wonder
how we eat
with only
two legs
and
so short-necked?[*]

---

[*] *Twiga* is Kiswahili for *giraffe*.

We chased the
zebra and wildebeests
from one shady grove
to another.
Each of our moves
cautiously calculated
and countered.
They watch
as we approach,
hoping, perhaps,
that a move to the right
or left
would let them hold
their square
so quietly settled.
One step too close,
they move
intimidating creatures
so easily
intimidated
by the two-legged
taking their
peace *en passant*.

If ever
they held
their spot,
checkmate!

It's clear that
traffic lanes
are merely suggestions,
and the real rule:

"Little things give way
to bigger things."

Sometimes the road
takes its own course,
opening ruts to make
large and small
dance and circle–
midgets and giants,
dik-diks and
elephants
at the water hole
here in the road.

Speed Bumps

The pavement
draws them
from dirt paths,
and here
traffic passes with
shillings in the pockets
of drivers
becoming the life of
a man holding
roasted, but
slightly burned
ears of maize
in front of the windshield
bouncing with the syncopated
rhythm of the
speed bumps.
A woman guards
small stacks
of kindling
and dreams of salvation
from
someone else's fire
cooking
someone else's supper,
in an economy of coins
in a world
of bills.

Canna Lilies

Last summer
in our yard they
towered over my head
where hummingbirds made
pilgrimage to the
sweetness and drank
the flowers into
fat, brown seed pods
beneath each
withered bloom.

None of the
lilies in this
African garden
showed me any seed,
only flattened
scales
like shriveled eunuchs.

I asked the gardener
whose smile told me
my American fast-talk made
hearing difficult,
and my non-existent
Kiswahili
could not save me.
Yet,
he understood life
and saw my delight in his skill.
On the last day,
he carried
mother earth to me
in a plastic bag
where she held tight
and nursed
freshly dug, fleshy
tubers.

At home
I root them away from
winter's freeze,
gathering them in crates,
refugees confined
to cellar's darkness.
But in this
Kenyan garden all
seeds are surrendered
as soil holds on to
life without
fear of frost.

I took his sack
and his smile
rehearsing in my mind
the sleight-of-hand
to leave roots
behind,
and yet carry
his gift.

Not all immigrants
find welcome
in a country populated
by wanderers[*]
and I return
to the seeded world
as he tends
the source.

---

[*] original meaning of *mzungu*, people who went in circles

The Great Rift Valley

Some things are
too big to be fenced
in syllables,
too ancient
for language,
and here
it lies.

256 Zones of Gray

Earth

Rain is an excuse
I didn't want to use so
I went out into
the filter of cloud,
a day imitating Ansel Adams with
256 zones of gray,
each a color of its own,
each distinct,
each alive,
and crisp,
and clear.
The autumn foliage
plots to cheat the day
with muted pigment,
but light doesn't allow it.
Water, sky, tree, grasses
full of color, yet not.
Silver water beads on waxy leaves.
I won't sit on the park bench today,
but stand at the juncture of black and white,
in the cast of muted light,
in the spectrum filtered sky.

I spit in the river like a boy,
but nobody saw me,
I made sure of that.
I was dry
after running across the field,
with lungs heaving
and mouth powdery.
It was like that, and I stopped
on the bridge to quench my thirst
by staring at the water.

So I spit.

It was white and chalky swirling
in black water till it caught the
current and was lost in the foam
over rocks and broken twigs.
I watched beyond what I saw,
and no one else saw or spoke except
a catbird on the railing.

I spit in the river like a boy

Xanthophyll, anthocyanin, and carotene
how clinical the pigments sound
shunning mystery for accuracy.

How stunning in autumn sunlight
as the greens surrender
and the trees put on
yellow, red, and orange,
colors a child could name.

Burial Ground

The really old cemeteries
forget themselves,
attracting only the living,
and not the dead.
In this field where no grass
has been uprooted
for seasons uncounted,
the departed already have,
and new generations refuse to gather.

Genealogists come,
but do not stay.
They read the stones
as if deciphering
glyphs of an ancient race
while sandstone defies
its carver by giving up letters.
Halloween brings the fearful,
afraid of the wrong things.
They come to the safety
of abandoned bodies
telling such tales of fright
that only living hands could accomplish,
and those hands are present here no longer.

If a murderous fist
with axe and blade were here,
long time has passed since
malice crossed mind
or will drove the fatal strike.
Some cry out to leave them alone,
as though bothering them was in our power.
"Let the dead be!" they say.

"Be what?" I ask. "Dead?"
Is there some other form of substance
I could invoke upon them?
Happy?
Joyful?
Peaceful bliss?
Yes, the place has become peacefully empty,
but if there is more to give than words,
another arm than mine must do it.

The teacher named it
ROY G. BIV.
I didn't know any Roys,
except Rogers,
and never any Bivs,
but this was hardly a stranger
to those who asked
for the hall light
left on
and the door
open a crack.
Visible light,
always a friend,
but having edges
not just in darkness now,
but at "R" and "V".

The school nurse would
take us in groups
down the hall to a
small room,
six at a time.
There, in the hushed silence
of a violet glow,
she'd run a hand
through our hair
looking for lice.
It was the color of light
on the edge of light,
wondrous thing,
beauty at the end of BIV.
I always wanted to return
to that room
and look again,
over the edge of color.

Washburn Ditch

There's a place where the ditch
cuts under the highway
and great pipes carry the flow,
channeling the flood until
it bursts free meandering
to reclaim its older path.

From there, earth is cut away
by water snaking around
dipping under fallen trunks
sidling past the heaps of brush
that washed down from neighborhoods
on the other side of town.

Floating toys will take the ride
before fast grip can gather,
escaping backyards during
the sudden-rising storm surge.

Here in the wooded silence,
beyond the noisy traffic,
they pile up in the tangles
waiting rescue that won't come.
The squirrels take no notice,
and muskrat finds no delight.

In the purgatory
of lost objects they pass time
until other hands find them,
or greater floods send them on.

My last walk takes me along the highway,
a path so straight no four-legged creature would forge.
Nothing more than a train bed stripped of rail and tie,
trying to go wild.

Traffic floods my ears,
but not my eyes.
Walls of tree and shrub
rise towering left and right
like Charlton Heston at the Red Sea,
not Moses at the *yam suph*,
an adventure without special effects.

This path is becoming real
with howling wind and shaking boughs.
Birds gone to cover flushed at my approach,
but this is their place now.
I, the invader, who did not come to conquer.

A trail of lasts,
last blue chicory staring up from swirling leaves,
last of the sumacs' red foliage with
cone-shaped parapets guarding the flank,
monarchs too weak for Mexico looking for
the last of the milkweed.
And the berries of white and blue and red,
Dogwood, grapes, haw, and a fruit
so red-ripe a grownup would warn against tasting.
Boys deserve such warnings,
fears grow slower than feet.
These last grapes were small
too bitter, I thought, but still, I tasted
sour and mostly seed from a summer beyond dry.
A boy would eat them,
one who had sworn a childhood oath to run away.
The clan would never be broken.
We would escape to the woods
eating berries and fruits like woodland tribes.

These last fruits belong to others now,
to birds lying hunkered in the bushes,
the worst eaten last,
fruit for desperation of a spring delayed.

Groundhog

There was a groundhog on the trail,
dead,
without any visible marks,
still.
The road runs so close
he could have been bluntly struck
only to race this far,
not knowing the death he carried
in his body.
Knowing, he might have preferred
to die here in a place of solitude
without fume
waiting for me to walk by.

Maybe my imagination plays tricks
and he came gently to this
spot to sleep,
stepping out of his body
as a friend of death
recognizing what
he and I have always carried in our bodies
and taking the lighter path.

It's colder this morning as I walk toward the river.
Not so cold, yet, that the trees have shaken color.
That comes later and I will wade knee-deep
through the discarded fabric of their splendor.

It isn't wind that robs them; they surrender freely.
Through summer gale I have seen them grip petiole
against any onslaught, but once the dimming day
sends the chill,
they push them off to flutter down in silence.
Even a still day sees them quietly relinquish
what they held so severely against the blast.

It is the cold that drives this barren cause.
Then they turn to cheat the freeze with branches so bare
that winter's fury can't grasp. Stripped of all but self,
they cast slim shadows of wind and light.
Foliage will bloom again in spring fashion,
but twig and branch are life and not dropped easily.
They do not think or feel, I am told,
but pruned, they burst from new bud,
as if nurtured by wound and pain,
purpose without intention, life from earth.

Along the Shore

The trees along the shore
took off their green
and the sky threaded
a blue ribbon between the trunks.

Fall is a season of paths
where spaces open through
the underbrush and the
wooded wall becomes a way.

Winter is so much softer
when I see it from my window.
The furnace comes on with a cool draft
in advance of heated air.
It's not the chill of real wind
that sets the teeth rattling
and skin to rise,
every hair alert.
Real winter is just beyond the pane
and I watch, hardly touched by it.
Even with hand on glass I sense the cold
but do not enter it,
or hardly enter.
Such a warm game to watch the winter,
pretending to be there
in shirtsleeves
observing swirling snow,
but not knowing any of it.

Wakefield

There were
tracks in the new snow
(a squirrel most likely
by the way he'd
hopped from
one drift
to another)
I mused over following
the imprints to
where they ended
perhaps with a frozen corpse
or warm leaf-den
stranded on bare limbs.
I gave up the idea
figuring I'd lose him
in the spring or
under newer snow.

Not Like Jesus

River is frozen
in sunlight the gulls gather
ice shines like white sand.

Cat creeps on the frosted flood.
Walks on water–not Jesus.

Sky

The last time I spoke with the moon,
it gave me no answer.
"What makes you so smug?" I said.
Nothing came but the silvery wash of silence.
It was fully awake, but even a canine's howl
    could not entice speech from it.

What taunt could touch this lesser light?
"The sun would answer," I chided.
(But I knew that I would never willingly
    look into that face.)
The moon knew too as it lulled along its silent path.

"You listen, but you do not speak!"

Nothing.

"If you spoke, I would listen!"

Nothing.

"If we both spoke, neither could listen!"

Nothing.

"If we both listened, neither would speak!"

"I hear it too."

The silvery wash of silence.

Under Sail

The water talks to me
in measured rhythms
of wave against hull.
Its beat stirs a gull
from her fascination
with a floating meal.
She has been wary of my approach,
wondering how close I will come,
or if my desire is for her prize.
The white sails are my wings,
but I am bound to the intersection
of wind and wave;
I can go no higher.
Gull knows my earthbound frame.
Grudgingly she unfolds her arms
mounting up, embracing sky.
She takes to air, circles the mast,
and sets down in her place.
She cries out to tell me
I am only an annoyance.
Her voice syncopates the
rhythm of the water.

My Sky

When I look up,
the sky is mine.
It is no bigger than I
because it can
be caressed and held close
like a lover,
and still bigger
so that freedom is
soaring in hot currents
where there are no
directions, no course plotting,
no up or down or
earth to abort life.
Just sky,
to be touched
and molded until
its breath is mine
and my lungs hold in
blue air
then let it go
to run after with
new life.

Morning

It is morning,
and the deck is wet with dew.
The air is crisp
and my life opens in the silence.
A Great Blue wades along the near shore.
At first,
I think he is watching me,
then, not.
His neck swiftly uncoils
and he's snared
a shiny fish.
He takes a new stance.
So still, he stands between
energy and matter,
between flashes of lightning reaction
and the serene pause.
Then it is finished.
He opens his wings and lifts to the sky
more pteranodon than avian.
He tips on the wind and I nod back.
It is morning,
and the deck is wet with dew.
My life opens in the silence.

Flight

From my cell, I see the clouds,
but feel no wind,
no breath to wash me clean.
Falcon is not envious of fume or power,
but I of her,
For she wings free, soaring with silent strokes
in an ocean of air.

What does she see?
Is it hare or mouse or shadow of light?
Can she see beyond the light,
and glimpse her own circle of self?

Falcon is no dreamer, she just wings free,
and in that, is more wise than I,
with fewer fears and no remorse.

But does she love?
And if love bears the price of other emotions,
I will love,
I will fly free,
I will soar as Falcon in an ocean of air.

The Turning

The geese are calling
early this year, and
urging
sluggish wings to flight after a
season of gleaning fatness from the fields.
They protest as they mount upward,
then fall into rhythm
with one voice
calling a cadence
for beating wings.
Their complaints
fall away
in precise formation.
The season changes.

Cat on the Ice

A cat walks
on the frozen river
her big belly
swollen with kittens.
They cry out hungrily within
as she watches gulls
standing à la mode.
I call to her;
She hunkers down.
Distrust is the edge of survival.
Lives on instinct
and birds
slow to flight

Along an open stretch of sandy shore
two brothers breathed the dream of human flight.
With canvas-covered frame they stood before
the wind which lifted time and forward sight
in views unseen by an earth-bound race.
What fears were theirs who gravity defied
whether stretched on wing or standing in place?
The toss of a coin determined the ride,
but both held forth that day to trust unknown.
They saw the work of hand and mind revealed
when engine sang and wings lifted over foam
in birdless flight with human fears concealed.
Earth flew on frail wing that December day
when sky became a place for human play.

Red Huffy

Pedaling with fury
of wheeling sprocket
racing downhill
adding muscle
to accelerating
free fall,
then standing
full height
levitating on pedals
above the earth,
hot air rising from
freshly rolled asphalt
becoming hot wind
rushing over
arms outstretched
in balance
without grip.
I am become
the cyclist
who invented flight.
My brother
only watches with envy
as my red Huffy
blurs in a jetting
streak of imagination.

Sky 'ku

perched jay
calling for peanuts
watching cat

town sleeps
under icy-white sky
smiling moon

sky opens
water overflows the curb
looking for the pond

Time

Black Hole

So dense even light cannot escape
sucking everything into its gravity
pulling all variety of matter
into one dot of space.
Time compresses into a thing,
one thing
with everything else,
real,
solid,
one.
Until, with word of power
all light is scattered,
one becomes many,
energy becomes matter,
time begins.

Bill had a watch
and an airplane made out of a white bull's horn.
The watch in his pocket,
the plane in a corner cupboard
behind glass shutters
where a boy could not reach.

Bill was a mystery,
my Gammy's husband with my last name,
but not a grandfather.
Gammy said his real name was Polish,
but took the name "Smith."
More American, he thought.

My Grandpa Smith
came from Glasgow
and called the name "Scottish."
He was always a stranger,
probably a watch in his pocket, too
but buried before my father was nine.

Bill's watch was not gone.
It came out like
a magic talisman,
always a delight
at the end of a chain.
Beneath the shiny cover,
a white face with crisp black features,
X, V, and I's.

For years I wore a watch on a wrist
shackled to time.
Now, like a smooth stone,
time lives in my pocket.
I open it
and look into its eye,
not to see it,
but to be connected,
to Bill, to Gammy,
to a bull's horn that looked like
it might fly.

Night Train

Darkness meets darkness
at the glass wall that divides
the still black of the sleeping travelers
from the glittering smooth,
ebony world that slides
past with clatter of wheels.

The night wanders free
consuming light and life,
while two steel bars stretch
to pull me their captive.

I open the window.

A different blackness meets
stale air,
and the smell of the land
becomes my breath.
The night is a part of me.

I sleep, then wake.

In the distance
a single lighted window,
and for a moment
I shared that light,
and the rails,
and then the darkness.

I am old enough to remember clocks
that ticked at night,
lying in bed,
sleepless.
Their beat was the interminable
drumming of a distant
enemy mocking my consciousness,
or the sometimes steady
drip, drip, drip
of a Chinese water torture
that drives mad and ends all hope of dreaming.
There is no ticking tonight,
just the faint green glow of the digital face.
My eyes,
so adjusted to the dark,
see shadows cast on the wall
by its glimmer.
Ticking was, at least a voice,
a companion in its time,
reminding me of the moments sliding helplessly away.
Tonight time flows silently
sleuthing away hours,
slowly without a cadence
that counts the tasks left undone.
By day, it flies.
Yet, from day to day, so little seems to change
and I am back under the green glow.
Sometimes I think that time doesn't change anything
until I see myself in the mirror.
I will not fight this time.
Like the child's game,
it will come,
ready or not.

| Time |

Keep it.
Mark it.
Save it.
Do as you like,
but the words do not fit
and prove false.
It will not hold the stain
when marked,
never kept on a string,
or pocketed with change.
Not ours forever.
Keeps us.
Marks us,
passes us into the ages.

How different today,
parking on Mount Washington,
taking the Incline down into the valley.
The old train station is now a boutique mall;
the waitress at lunch laughed easily.

Coming back,
the sky framed a perfect postcard
with colors sliding back into the rivers
to define the Point.

No smoke in the valley.
Not like the days when my grandfather
rode this track into smoldering
steam from the mills,
fume of open hearth,
the descent into hell.

The laborers came back up,
armed with black lunch pails already emptied
into hungry stomachs,
faces darkened with sweat-molded soot.

It was work, not penance
that took them down to the coke fires,
and obstinate pride that lifted them back
at shift's end.

I remember her much taller
than she was.
Of course, I was only six
and everyone was tall
except my little brother.
In the pantry was a calendar with a beautiful princess
crowned with tiara
face framed with rosy cheeks,
but no longer a princess,
Elizabeth, her royal highness.
My grandmother was Elizabeth, too,
her only claim to royalty,
a sister
a cook's assistant at Balmoral.
At Grandma's house
another form of
nurture reigned.
To lost boys came
biscuits from brightly colored tins,
white tea,
and buttery shortbreads.

The kitchen was bright and sunny
on the second floor.
In the hall,
a picture of a Sunday school class.
My class.
I remember the day it was taken,
and why I sat
so angelically
next to teacher
while others
played to the camera
or ran amok.
Donnie, Billy, Glen, and Wendy
the names of childhood friends
nearly gone from memory.

My mother dressed me for that picture,
not without protest,
wearing white shirt, bowtie,
    open jacket, short pants,
        and Buster Browns.

I hated wearing shorts.
Men did not wear them,
why should I at four?
I didn't want my picture taken,
knees bared in so unmanly a way.
I sat by the teacher,
out of center.
"Out," teacher said, "of the camera's eye."
She had lied in church that day,
the day I sat on the outside of my own world
and watched children being children
while I sat as a man,
bare-kneed and alone.
I don't know if my mother ever saw the photo.
In time, it came to define me in the Grandma world,
but so did the biscuits and tea
and the wey
she sang tae us,
"Lizbeth."

Fear

As a child
I did not appreciate fear.
Oh, there were
baby fears
of dark basements
haunted by hulking
furnaces with
long arms of gravity-fed
cold air returns.
They were just pipes
and shadows.
They did not hit like the Toughs
who thought me a small, safe target.
Only twice did
any land the stinging blow.
I remember their reactions,
both the same,
though years apart.
I must not have done it right,
not to suit them.
After straight shot to face,
they stopped
heads turning to silent companions,
as if their attempt at improvisation
had left the story-line.
I failed the audition.
Was I to fall?
or cry?
or run?
Like an idiot,
I did nothing.
They should have told me.
I just stood my ground
and they wondered if I had
seen the stars.
I had,
but not enough to appreciate fear.

No second punch ever found me,
and the two traced
wide circles around me after that
as if I knew the secret of
their souls,
the boy who didn't
fall,
or fight,
or run.
In time, fear found me.
I see the ones I love
at a distance
where fate makes helpless.
Easier to take the blow
and stand-down
the bully.

No Time for Angst

My first car was a Rambler,
flathead six,
mostly rust
when I took its wheel.
But the front seat flipped
down into a bed,
not that I needed it
for submarine races,
still,
there in case.
Angst was not making it
with grades,
with girls,
and Nam was in the headlines
and the back of nineteen-year-old minds.
It was not assumed
that things would break right
if the cash was good,
or mommy and daddy made it so.
Rights were opposites of lefts,
and choice was to please the Dean
or go to Uncle.
Do or die.
Many did both.
No time for angst,
just choices.

Karl's Barber shop was a man's place
with an inviolate code of conduct.
Each knew his place in the rotation.
"First in, first up" was the only rule,
and "Next" was the call to the plate.
Karl and Joe umpired the procession,
and boys could play, their bikes leaning
against the brick wall in the alley.
The barber pole twisted red, white, and blue,
and rotating chrome chairs dangled straps
for honing razor's straight edge with
rhythmic slap of steel on leather.
Fearless Fosdick stared down from
comic posters, hat tipped, hair slicked,
and bullet holes with hovering flies.

My wife and I now go together,
there's a list to sign as we walk in.
The room smells of scratch and sniff roses
that live in a pile of magazines.
No greaseless Wildroot,
but an apricot/peach something.
Cassie doesn't look like a barber,
prettier than Karl without talk of
fish, football, or the eighth inning.
The time here is not the same,
not better or worse, just different,
a different thing altogether.

The Bonapartes landed
shaking off their black crowns
for winter plumage.
The Ring-bills wonder how long they will stay,
So do I
as the world becomes sleepy.
It will be a fitful sleep
with the children off to war.
The gulls are not sleeping.
They make a mess of the empty docks
and sit in their army array,
Ring-billed and Bonaparte
waiting for a Waterloo
or another migration.
Yesterday, I saw a Coot swimming
near the edge of the basin
passing itself off as a duck,
minding its own business.
Too bad about the name.
Holy in its way.

Last Dance

I saw a man stop dancing.
It was at the bar and a band was playing,
a good band.
The regulars came to dance
and drink,
and laugh,
and make up stories
that got bigger
with the amplified beat of the bass guitar.
An older man was there,
not much older.
He had come to dance

All in black,
two-tone shoes,
silver buckle
he had the moves.
He and his partner did not miss a step
until
he just stopped.
Would have gone down hard
but for the woman in his arms
who gently floated at his side.
Dance floor suddenly clear
and the squad repeating
"Clear."
Three times they shocked him
before sliding him onto a body board,
gurneying him out the door
He had come to dance.

Plato's Forms (a pantoum)

beyond words, beyond time
truth can be seen without eyes
what is seen is true
knowledge without perspective

truth can be seen without eyes
senses no longer distort
knowledge without perspective
truth stands eternal

senses no longer distort
subjective self is gone
truth stands eternal
as it was, is, and will be

subjective self is gone
what is seen is true
as it was, is, and will be
beyond words, beyond time

Patterns

Memento, homo, quia pulvis es et in pulverem reverteris[*]

Memento

Memento,
Remember the days of dust
when no smell was sweeter
than wet, black earth.
When babes
stepped forward out of the
dust of sand castles,
and the sun baked
the fortress
white and sugary.

Reverteris,
that's the trick.
Remembering counts too little.
It's the going back
that's tough.

Memento — Revererteris.
Reverteris — Memento.
Walk the castles carefully.
Sugar is weak mortar
and the bucket-molded towers
don't remember;
they just revert.
We walk the ledges
'til the sweetness
between our toes
becomes the weak enemy,
and there's nothing
to separate feet from enemy.
The seam disappears.
Man — Dust
Dust - Man

I am the wet ground.
The dust will remember.

---

[*] *Remember, man, thou art dust and to dust you will return*

Mandala

Today I was caught up
in a moment when it seemed
that I could touch the earth
and feel that it was
ready to be touched and
formed and moved
until it took a shape that
was not its own,
but an idea
that could count all things
as one,
and yet be everything.
Nowhere was this any more visible
than on the horizon.
Whether I stood back or close,
all was near,
flowing in a
singular separateness
that divided nothing,
not even time,
but made eternal moments
held by the
vastness of space
and the finitude of mind.

With new awareness I felt this,
and when eternity ended,
the moments slid
apart and I was left
in a shadow
while life called with
the voices heard in dreams.

Catbird, what will be new tomorrow?
Will brown sky meet us?
Will we call it new,
or call it sky?
No new sky.
"Tomorrow is today a day later,"
so calls the bird
with yesterday's song
and voice sweet enough
to make earth weep.
Wind speaks to tree,
tree to earth,
earth finds comfort,
but the word is not new.
Earth hears it well
and sends shoots to
pierce sky with wing and flight.
No new sky.
One child new,
only one.
Enough
Bird, sky, tree, earth, shoots, wing, child.
I will be new.
All are new.

I didn't know you
except after death,
and for this I'm glad
because now life won't
prove me wrong
when I try to remember
what you ought to have been.

Let's let that be for now,
you, the product of my creation
and me, the product of yours.
Apart from us, we really don't exist,
unless someone else has remembering,
but from what I've seen,
the world forgets,
and then I'm no better
for opening my eyes and making
your life go.
Then I'm all that's left
and there's not enough to
fill the living for two that
must be in one.

Strange how life and death
follow patterns that can't
be followed by the eye,
but only by the forgetting
and the remembering.
And if forgotten,
we're dead.
Unless someone else can recall
the numbers of hair
and the living we kept in our minds.

The elements of the universe
know nothing
of their being,
and yet, they speak of being.
They exist as a word that is spoken,
a word so real that
all other voices
seem muted.
My silence in all this seems
unnatural. For being endowed
with heart
and mind, lips and tongue,
I speak less eloquently,
with less faith and vigor,
but perhaps not with less hope.
For it is within hope I find
true humanity, and join
in the silent speech
of the created order.

Persephone rides on laughter.
Her beauty brings the spring,
her playfulness carries the
scent of new grass.

Had I wondered where laughter went,
I should have known when I
went searching for the friend of my youth.
For in you it breathes so easily,
like the spring,
like the scent of new grass.
Wander with me
fair and free
through meadows,
and along fresh paths,
until the laughter greets us
and our hearts are one.

More Tests

They want more tests
to test the results of the last test
that might not be right.
The tests never make well.
They sow fright to make themselves important
and everything hinges on them.
Joy is getting word that nothing was found.
Six months, test again,
maybe three (just to be safe!)
Of course, nothing is our latest hope.
Life is managing the spaces between
the nothing and the may be
something.

Fear is the driver,
fear of death.
Who named him that,
the one who has always walked beside?
Do they think tests can chase him off
or have they been merely counting laps to the finish,
waiting for a checkered flag?
Death is the faithful companion,
the one never-forsaking friend,
always has been.
I carry him in me.
He is my teacher who tells me to live until
there is only one
next reasonable step
over the invisible threshold.

Some take another roll,
hedging bets with a test.

Machines feed well on fearful flesh.

Without Purpose

I am going to learn to walk without purpose,
to stop halfway down the sidewalk
and talk to myself
with animated gestures.
I will always linger long enough
so that everyone who views
the surveillance camera
knows that I have no cell phone.
Someday they will all know me
In the malls,
parking lots,
and public buildings.
"Poor bastard," they will call me,
"Harmless," too.
They will ask each other
if I have gone off my medication,
or if I have ever been truly diagnosed.
Seeing me thus,
they will cease to see me at all.
I suppose watching neighbors
is always easier than knowing.
In the end, the spectators
are deluded.

Pantoum of Time

wild geese fly overhead
reminding me of the time
season will soon change
winter comes on the wing

reminding me of the time
reminding me of times gone past
winter comes on the wing
new days of graying skies

reminding me of times gone past
time I lost in sorrow
new days of graying skies
winter brings the spring

time I lost in sorrow
season will soon change
winter brings the spring
wild geese fly overhead

Fingernail Moon

A fingernail moon
held its place
in the deep darkness of the sky.
Its paralyzing
half-light held
all things silent,
waiting for a sound
to engulf creation
in a tempestuous power
that would burst
into irreversible history.

Finally, the hush fell away,
a breeze welled up
and soothed
the land
like a cool breath
mumbling,
"not tonight."

Eucharist

Life comes,
with no holding on.
We see and feel
until the aching for it
lifts it from the table.
There is no drinking,
only seeing.
"I thirst," cries a voice,
but lips are weak arms.
The cup is too high,
too shiny,
and the polish burns against
raw flesh.
The only drink is tears and sweat,
the only cup the sunken eyes
and cheeks.

The drink is in the thirsting.
Life is not held,
only let go.

Covenant with the Dead

To Edith

Death came long, but suddenly,
and now it doesn't matter
because our secret is kept
and there'll be no more telling.

But then I told you
it would be that way,
and you seemed pleased
that one so young
would know a tale of the old.

So now you're past dying,
but I am left
the bearer of half a secret.
Your half's still good
though I heard a whisper of it
when you left.
No bother though,
it's still safe,
or will be
when I come across.

Wandering in mazes of our own making,
we stumble in places we did not choose.

The twists of the labyrinth
set us swimming in confusion,
one path turns into two,
then disappears into a solid wall.

Was there not a time
when this was a child's game?
A riddle to be solved,
a problem clothed in boxwood hedges
for an afternoon's delight?

In that garden was laughter,
and a key to the puzzle.
What was it?
Keep a hand against the wall,
and the path will not turn
back on itself.
Was that it?

But the walls of this maze play tricks,
and a hand would not rest well against them.
A hand to hold would serve better.
Here's mine.

The night seemed longer than usual
and still no word
had come to them.
So they waited for
sign or sound,
but the streets were silent
and empty.
The children were in bed, but not
dreaming of sugarplums,
just dreaming.
The air was still
and hot and mixed with the smell of the
closeness of life,
and the emptiness of the streets echoed the silence.

A new baby cried
for the first time.
The night air
still hung heavy over the town,
but now the emptiness of the streets
echoed the cry.

Hope comes in a wooden box,
and it came
crying because there was
no one to pay
for being born,
so dying,
or living became the
payment.

Other than that
there was nothing
except the
scared
bunch
that left him standing
on a hill
with nothing to do
but take whatever came,
wine or spit.

I can't remember more.
He came in a wooden box
and we tried
to send him out the same way.
Some say there was a
mix-up
and he didn't leave at all.

The sunlight dances
through the shadows of the leaves
and is richer for touching
your cheek.
You laugh,
and I am richer
for sitting beside you.
How can I delight so
in my friend?
Yet, the sun delights
as the light dances on your cheek,
and I for touching you softly.

The sunlight dances

Love

There's an electric motor in my toothbrush.
It drones at me when it needs to be recharged,
and I obey more than the hygienist's plea
to floss regularly.
She knows well
that I do not,
but she always asks, and
I rinse and spit myself clean for six more months.
The motor shakes my jaw like a jackhammer
and offers no forgiveness
when I answer back.

Alzheimer

He looked at her voice,
For there he hoped to recognize her.
Dim eyes betray awareness,
But the voice was still real.
Names no longer matter,
Gone with all faces.

He looked at her voice.

Familiar, comforting, without face or name.

He looked at her voice,
But not as one tracing the wispy breath of a cold morning,
Those were images of sight,
They belonged to the eyes.

When memory and vision fade,
one only sees with the ears and remembers with the heart.

He looked at her voice.

What was it? It was familiar, it was safe.

"Don't worry, I'm here!"

Beginnings,
are they really new?
Or do we carry our old selves along
until we feel new and fresh and alive?
How does the journey start?
With a laugh,
or a tear,
or with hands touching
so lightly that we fear they will
let go.

My hands are strong enough to hold,
and gentle enough to catch a tear.

Already I feel new.
Is it a new beginning?

Beginnings

Escape to Poetry

The story nags at me as I sit at my desk.
The characters cry that they
long for life, for action,
and they tire of waiting for me.
I tell them to go ahead without me,
but they never do.
When I do sit with them, they won't listen.
They push me along when I want to linger
on a sunset or feel the burning run
of a line racing through bare hands.
"Hurry," they urge as if my fingers
could fly fast enough
to add pulse to their
already racing hearts.
What do they want from me besides life?
"It's a small thing," they argue,
but it sounds like nagging to me.
They never do what I want
and the chapter leaves
them hanging less than me.
I swear that I love them,
but sometimes I betray,
secretly stealing myself away.
I make the excuses of a faithless partner,
"It's their fault, they demand so much,
day after day, they drive me to another," I say.
She will be kind and soft.
She makes no demands,
holds me in her arms,
and tells me how abused I am.
I want to receive her words,
and, even more, the way of her touch.
"Just a few short lines," she whispers,
not even asking me to speak her name.
We meet only in the discretion
of a quiet time together
when the world of senses
overwhelms self

and we are alone,
without the voices,
without the nagging,
without the story.
Just poetry.

(a pantoum)

Darfur

Being born human,
compassion should come easy
as my kin sit in the waste of war,
sisters and brothers of one flesh.

Compassion should come easy,
but I live in isolation of
sisters and brothers of one flesh,
voices calling in need.

But I live in isolation of
soft music that covers their cry,
voices calling in need
I, who have ears to hear.

Soft music covers their cry
as my kin sit in the waste of war
I, who have ears to hear,
being born human.

Milkweed

A child running,
arms flailing
 to catch the drifting seed,
the Santa Claus seed
as light as a feather,
as white as the snow.

In cupped hands
the treasure rests,
framed by soft fingers
darkened by the sootiness
of boy-play.

Now he whispers the wish
beyond his power to secure,
the magical words now risked to
be spoken aloud.

Then upward he flings his hands,
the swirling puff circles,
drifts,
and catches currents.
Without sound,
beyond sight,
it is gone.

Whatever became of the hopes of a boy?

Have they become
the food of caterpillars,
the shelter of a chrysalis,
the stalk for the unfolding
of wet sticky wings?
Or is the whisper of magic
that takes its own wings,
and drifts and floats until
it finds another hand to hold it?
Another heart to listen?

She asked me what I thought,
but long ago,
I knew that I would like her.
Should I tell her,
tell her that her eyes
say more about her heart
than she might want this stranger to know?

She asked me what I thought
about the clutter of a room,
but I see only ties to friends
at a distance,
that she holds on to love,
and her eyes say more
than she might want this stranger to know.

I wonder what she thinks,
when I call for no reason
except to hear her voice?
Long ago,
I knew that I would like her,
but does she see, in my eyes, more
than I might want this stranger to know?

Truth Aloud

Words without feelings
are sounds to be heard and
nothing more.
If woven in syllables alone,
the artist may be seen.
If crafted in beauty,
the skill is discerned,
but without feeling the heart
remains unknown.
A lie spoken beautifully remains untrue.
A truth unspoken may starve a hungry soul.
So I offer the truth,
plainly spoken,
without craft or skill:
I am a man.
I love you.

Love's Shades of Gray *

In 2011, composer R. Michael Daugherty created a musical setting for these five poems. The resulting song cycle was first recorded by Marguerite Krull, soprano, and Craig Ketter, pianist.

*BIOGRAPHICAL SKETCH: "Dr. R. Michael Daugherty is well known as a composer. His compositions include over sixty songs and over fifty choruses. He has also written three string quartets and various pieces for orchestra, band, assorted chamber ensembles and solo instruments that have been heard in hundreds of performances throughout the eastern United States and in at least eight European countries."

SOURCE: American Composers Forum (www.composersforum.org)

Beyond horizons,
the sun rises and sets.
Beyond horizons,
the eyes wander until
the unseen takes shape,
and the world is formed.

To speak of things unseen is to dream.
Dreams are the mother of hope,
and her children are my sisters.
Dreams birth the colors of a new dawn,
and the dawn is my brother.

Why should I fear my brother,
or my sister?
Am I not also a child of dreams?

I stand at the dawn.
My heart holds hope.
My life speaks the dream.

If I scare you,
come closer,
and let me hold you.
There are many paths
that we could walk,
many ways to travel.
To choose one or another
matters less
than walking together.
Dreams are better
hand in hand,
your hand
and my hand.
Does this scare you?
Come closer,
love casts out fear.

I met our neighbor today
at the convenience store.
I was for coffee,
she, for scratching a lottery card.
Anyway, she asked if we were rich
just blurted it out,
like she always does
straight-out.

I must have smiled,
mostly at the predictable bluntness.
Next week she'll ask again
not remembering the old path,
but she took the smile as a "Yes"
so I had to question,
"What does it mean to be rich?"

Turning nosiness into philosophy is an art
I don't possess,
but what does it mean?
We don't owe much.
We eat so that we mind the scales
and walk off calories.
I know enough rich people.

In big houses they talk poor
as they try to gather more.
Still, it feels as if we have enough
just with each other.
So if you hear the rumor that we're rich,
it's gossip.
Probably true.

If we were children, would the world even wonder
As we walked together?
Would anyone notice our laughter, except for a
smiling sky and shapeless clouds
amused as we pointed at each wisp and spoke a name?

There is still a child in me.

If we were children, would the world even wonder
As minutes ticked into hours,
and the silence between words sang for joy?
Would either of us mourn the missed suppers?
The street lights awakened as daylight slips into night?
The shroud of darkness, and the stars that smile?

There is still a child in me.

If we were children, would the world even wonder
if I took your hand for a moment?
There is so much to see that is new,
so much to see that is fresh and undiscovered and true.
Or are you the one who is fresh, and undiscovered, and
true?

Do not laugh that I see you like this,
Children see everything differently.

There is still a child in me.

The flesh of your thigh
feels warm beneath my touch.
My senses are awash
with the fragrance of our bodies' communion.
After the passion,
it is still you I love.

Afterwords

"Visit" is
such a small word.
I'm not sure
anyone *visits*
the Louvre.

More experience
than place,
room
    pouring
        into
           room,
and I wonder
if anything
remains
      in Egypt
   or Greece
or Italy.

Mona does her best
to smile,
everyone else
is in the
trance
seen in malls
a week before
Christmas.

Do you remember the night
that we whispered and held one another?
Each fearing to lose the other in the darkness of sleep,
we would not close our eyes
until the sun gave us another day,
and hands rested together as we walked
in that new light.

Do you remember that time?
Or does it live only in my imagination?

It is not far to the place of my imagining.
Lie close to me and whisper.
I will take you there.

About the Author

Rob Smith currently lives and writes on Ohio's north coast. He enjoys sailing, and when not working on his writing, he is refurbishing an 1850's house which was built by a ship's carpenter turned lighthouse keeper. (As an aside, in 1872 the house was purchased by the German Evangelical Church and served as its parsonage until 1904. During that time, church services were conducted in German. So, he actually lives in the immigrant's house!)

He is the author of six novels, but has received recognition for his poetry. In 2006 he won the Robert Frost Poetry Award given by the Frost Foundation in Lawrence, MA. He holds his undergraduate degree from Westminster College in Pennsylvania and master and doctoral degrees from Princeton Theological Seminary. *The Immigrant's House* is his third book of poetry.

To learn more about this author, visit his website at: SmithWrite.net

PHOTO CREDIT:
NANCY SMITH

CPSIA information can be obtained at www.ICGtesting.com
Printed in the USA
BVOW072312170712

295488BV00001B/39/P